Delicious Food
Color by Number for Adults
A Yummy Coloring Book for Relaxation

Color Questopia

Copyright © 2021

All rights reserved. No part of this publication may be reproduced, distributed, or transmitted in any form or by any means, including photocopying, recording, or other electronic or mechanical methods, without the prior written permission of the publisher

Our Color Palette Tips

1. **Colors corresponding to each number are shown on the back cover of the book - NEW- There are only 25 colors total in this book, with one "Flesh Tone" color where you can choose any flesh tone!**

   Each number corresponds to a color shown on the back of the book. **There will sometimes be an asterisk (*) that corresponds to "Any Flesh Tone."**
   To the left of each image, there's a list of colors used within that particular image. Simply match the numbers on the images to the colors on the list. If you tear a page out of the book, you can simply use the color key on the back of the book to match your colors. If you don't have an exact color match, that's totally fine. Feel free to use a similar color or shade. Although this is a color by number book, it's completely okay to get creative and change up the colors listed. You can let your imagination run wild, and color the images with whichever colors you like and have. The numbers are here to be a guide and to allow you to color without having to focus your energy on choosing colors.

2. **If there are any spaces on an image without a number, you can go ahead and leave that space white (blank)**

   You can leave any space without a number white (blank), or you can fill that space in with any color you like. Another idea is to color that space in with a white color (for example, if you'd like to use a shiny white or a different shade of white on an image.)

3. **Bonus Images may have a slightly different color palette**

   Because the bonus images are from previous books with slightly different color palettes, they may include colors that aren't on the back of this book. Simply match them the best that you can, or choose completely different colors if you like. You are the artist and you are allowed to relax and enjoy!

Color By Number Tips

1. **Relax and have fun**

   Let your cares slip away as you color the images. Take your time. Coloring is a meditative activity and there's no wrong way to do it. Feel free to color as you listen to music, watch TV, lounge in bed- do whatever relaxes you most! You can also color while you're out and about- on the train or at a cafe- take the book with you anywhere you go. Coloring is therapeutic and is great for stress relief and relaxation!

2. **Choose your coloring tools**

   Everyone has their favorite coloring markers, crayons, pencils, pens- even paints! Feel free to color with any tool that you like! If you choose markers or paints, we recommend putting a blank sheet of paper or cardboard behind each image, so that your colors don't run onto the next image.

3. **Test out your colors**

   Feel free to test out your colors on our Color Test Sheets at the back, and use our Custom Color Chart to make the color choices your own!

   Relax and Enjoy!

1. Black

2. Gray

4. Brown

5. Dark Brown

6. Tan

7. Peach

8. Red

10. Orange

11. Light Yellow

12. Yellow

13. Golden Yellow

15. Green

16. Dark Green

17. Aqua Green

18. Light Blue

19. Blue

2. Gray

4. Brown

5. Dark Brown

6. Tan

7. Peach

8. Red

9. Orange Red

10. Orange

12. Yellow

13. Golden Yellow

14. Light Green

15. Green

16. Dark Green

17. Aqua Green

19. Blue

22. Violet

23. Pink

2. Gray
3. Dark Gray
4. Brown
5. Dark Brown
6. Tan
7. Peach
8. Red
9. Orange Red
10. Orange
12. Yellow
14. Light Green
15. Green
16. Dark Green
17. Aqua Green
18. Light Blue

19. Blue
21. Lilac
22. Violet
23. Vivid Pink

2. Gray
4. Brown
6. Tan
7. Peach
8. Red
9. Orange Red
10. Orange
11. Orange
12. Light Yellow
13. Golden Yellow
14. Light Green
15. Green
17. Aqua Green
19. Blue
21. Lilac

22. Violet
23. Pink
24. Vivid Pink

2. Gray

3. Dark Gray

4. Brown

5. Dark Brown

6. Tan

7. Peach

8. Red

10. Orange

12. Yellow

14. Light Green

15. Green

16. Dark Green

18. Light Blue

19. Blue

21. Lilac

22. Violet

23. Pink

24. Vivid Pink

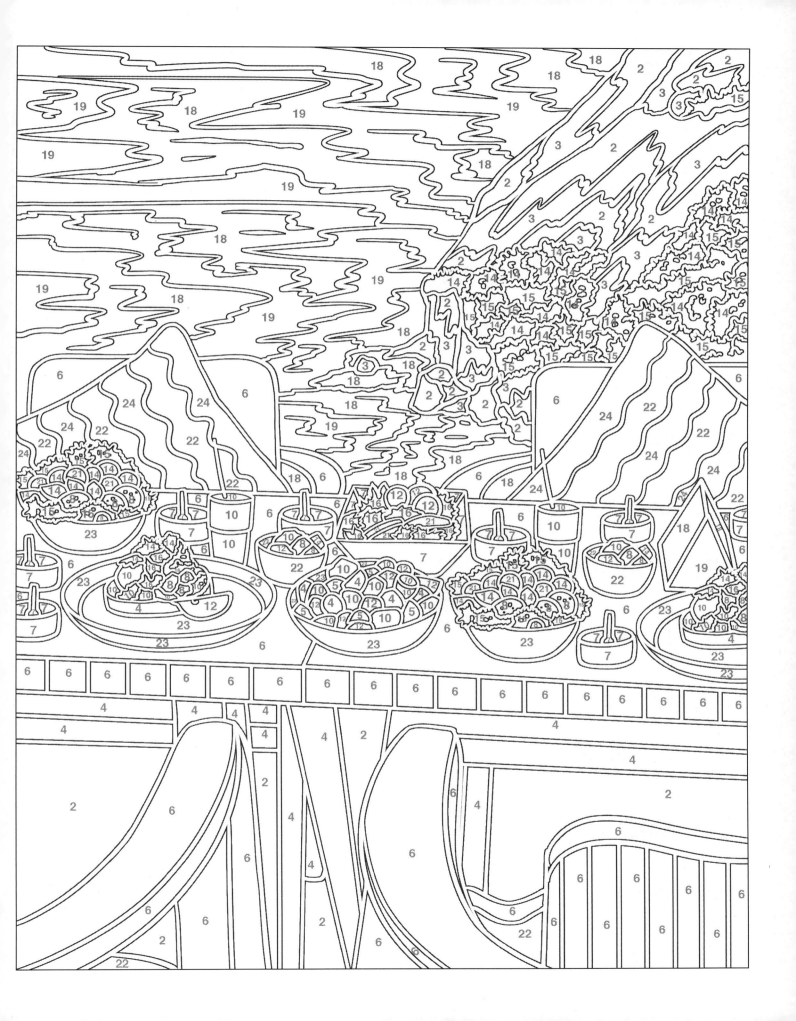

1. Black
2. Gray
4. Brown
5. Dark Brown
6. Tan
7. Peach
8. Red
11. Light Yellow
12. Yellow
15. Green
18. Light Blue
19. Blue
21. Lilac
22. Violet
23. Pink
24. Vivid Pink

1. Black
2. Gray
3. Dark Gray
4. Brown
5. Dark Brown
6. Tan
7. Peach
8. Red
10. Orange
11. Light Yellow
12. Yellow
13. Golden Yellow
14. Light Green
15. Green
18. Light Blue

19. Blue
21. Lilac
22. Violet
23. Pink
24. Vivid Pink

1. Black
2. Gray
4. Brown
6. Tan
7. Peach
8. Red
9. Orange Red
10. Orange
11. Light Yellow
12. Yellow
13. Golden Yellow
14. Light Green
15. Green
17. Aqua Green
21. Lilac

22. Violet
23. Pink
24. Vivid Pink

1. Black
2. Gray
4. Brown
6. Tan
7. Peach
8. Red
10. Orange
12. Yellow
13. Golden Yellow
14. Light Green
15. Green
17. Aqua Green
18. Light Blue
19. Blue
21. Lilac
22. Violet
23. Pink
24. Vivid Pink

4. Brown

6. Tan

7. Peach

8. Red

9. Orange Red

10. Orange

11. Light Yellow

12. Yellow

13. Golden Yellow

14. Light Green

15. Green

17. Aqua Green

22. Violet

23. Pink

24. Vivid Pink

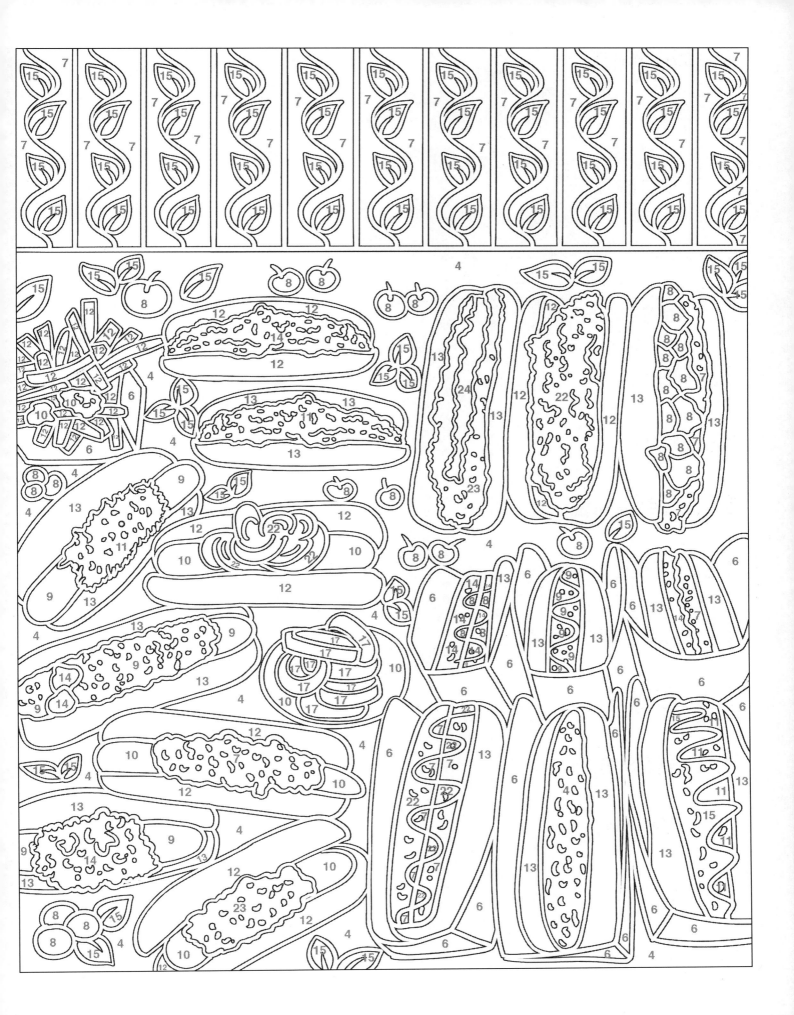

1. Black

2. Gray

4. Brown

5. Dark Brown

6. Tan

7. Peach

8. Red

10. Orange

11. Light Yellow

12. Yellow

14. Light Green

15. Green

16. Dark Green

18. Light Blue

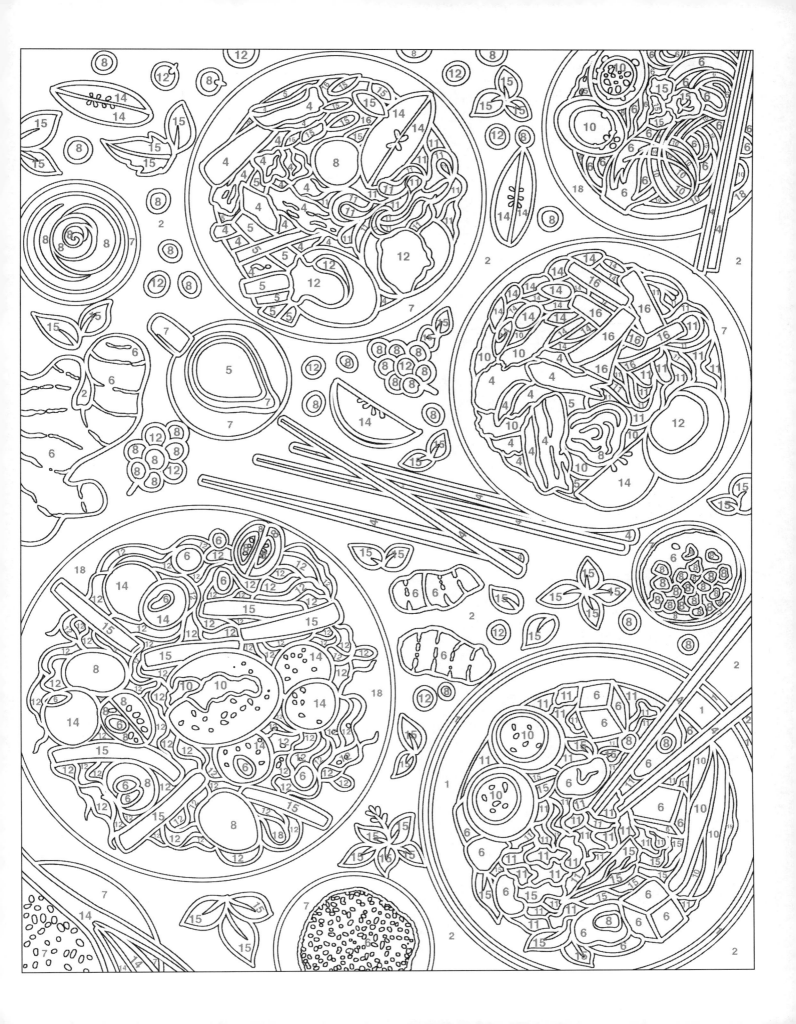

1. Black
2. Gray
3. Dark Gray
4. Brown
5. Dark Brown
6. Tan
7. Peach
10. Orange
11. Light Yellow
12. Yellow
14. Light Green
15. Green
17. Aqua Green
18. Light Blue
19. Blue

21. Lilac
22. Violet
23. Pink
24. Vivid Pink

2. Gray

3. Dark Gray

4. Brown

5. Dark Brown

6. Tan

7. Peach

8. Red

9. Orange Red

10. Orange

11. Light Yellow

12. Yellow

13. Golden Yellow

14. Light Green

15. Green

18. Light Blue

19. Blue

20. Dark Blue

21. Lilac

22. Violet

23. Pink

24. Vivid Pink

2. Gray

4. Brown

5. Dark Brown

6. Tan

7. Peach

8. Red

10. Orange

11. Light Yellow

12. Yellow

13. Golden Yellow

15. Green

17. Aqua Green

18. Light Blue

21. Lilac

2. Gray

4. Brown

5. Dark Brown

6. Tan

7. Peach

8. Red

9. Orange Red

10. Orange

12. Yellow

15. Green

17. Aqua Green

18. Light Blue

19. Blue

21. Lilac

22. Violet

2. Gray

4. Brown

6. Tan

7. Peach

8. Red

9. Orange Red

10. Orange

11. Light Yellow

12. Yellow

13. Golden Yellow

15. Green

17. Aqua Green

18. Light Blue

22. Violet

23. Pink

24. Vivid Pink

2. Gray

4. Brown

5. Dark Brown

6. Tan

7. Peach

8. Red

9. Orange Red

10. Orange

11. Light Yellow

12. Yellow

13. Golden Yellow

14. Light Green

15. Green

18. Light Blue

1. Black
2. Gray
4. Brown
6. Tan
8. Red
9. Orange Red
10. Orange
12. Yellow
13. Golden Yellow
14. Light Green
15. Green
16. Dark Green
17. Aqua Green
18. Light Blue
20. Dark Blue
22. Violet
23. Pink
24. Vivid Pink

2. Gray

3. Dark Gray

4. Brown

5. Dark Brown

6. Tan

7. Peach

8. Red

9. Orange Red

11. Light Yellow

12. Yellow

13. Golden Yellow

14. Light Green

15. Green

16. Dark Green

18. Light Blue

19. Blue

1. Black

2. Gray

4. Brown

5. Dark Brown

6. Tan

7. Peach

8. Red

9. Orange Red

10. Orange

11. Light Yellow

12. Yellow

13. Golden Yellow

15. Green

18. Blue

21. Lilac

23. Pink

2. Gray

4. Brown

5. Dark Brown

6. Tan

7. Peach

8. Red

12. Yellow

13. Golden Yellow

14. Light Green

15. Green

16. Dark Green

18. Light Blue

21. Lilac

22. Violet

23. Pink

1. Black

2. Gray

4. Brown

6. Tan

7. Peach

8. Red

11. Light Yellow

12. Yellow

13. Golden Yellow

14. Light Green

15. Green

16. Dark Green

1. Black
2. Gray
3. Dark Gray
4. Brown
5. Dark Brown
6. Tan
7. Peach
8. Red
9. Orange Red
10. Orange
11. Light Yellow
12. Yellow
13. Golden Yellow
15. Green
16. Dark Green

17. Aqua Green
18. Light Blue
21. Lilac

1. Black
2. Gray
3. Dark Gray
4. Brown
5. Dark Brown
6. Tan
7. Peach
8. Red
11. Light Yellow
12. Yellow
13. Golden Yellow
14. Light Green
15. Green
18. Light Blue
21. Lilac
22. Violet
23. Pink
24. Vivid Pink

1. Black
2. Gray
4. Brown
5. Dark Brown
6. Tan
7. Peach
8. Red
9. Orange Red
10. Orange
11. Light Yellow
12. Yellow
14. Light Green
15. Green
17. Aqua Green
19. Blue

20. Dark Blue
21. Lilac
24. Vivid Pink

ENJOY BONUS IMAGES FROM SOME OF OUR OTHER FUN COLOR BY NUMBER BOOKS!

FIND ALL OF OUR BOOKS ON AMAZON

Candy Coloring Book
Delicious Mosiac Color By Number
Sweet Treats and Desserts

1. Red
2. Light Red
3. Gray
4. Yellow
5. Light Yellow
6. Pink
7. Brown
8. Light Pink
9. Hot Pink
10. Light Green
11. Chocolate
12. Violet
13. Orange
14. Blue
15. Light Blue
16. Dark Gray
17. Peach

Chibi Girls
Volume 2
Color By Number
Coloring Book for Adults

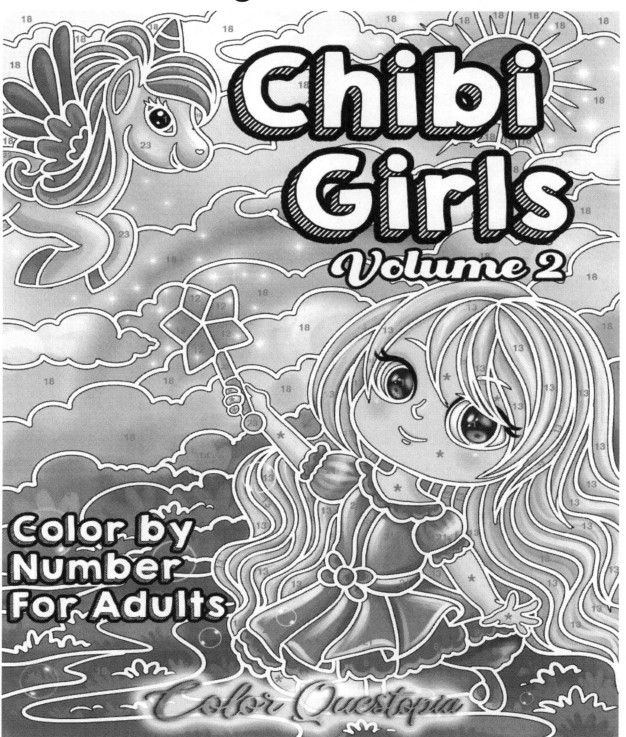

1. Black

2. Gray

3. Dark Gray

4. Brown

5. Dark Brown

6. Tan

7. Peach

8. Red

10. Orange

12. Yellow

17. Aqua Green

19. Blue

20. Dark Blue

22. Violet

23. Pink

24. Vivid Pink

*. Any Flesh Tone

Winter Mandalas
Color By Number
Coloring Book for Adults

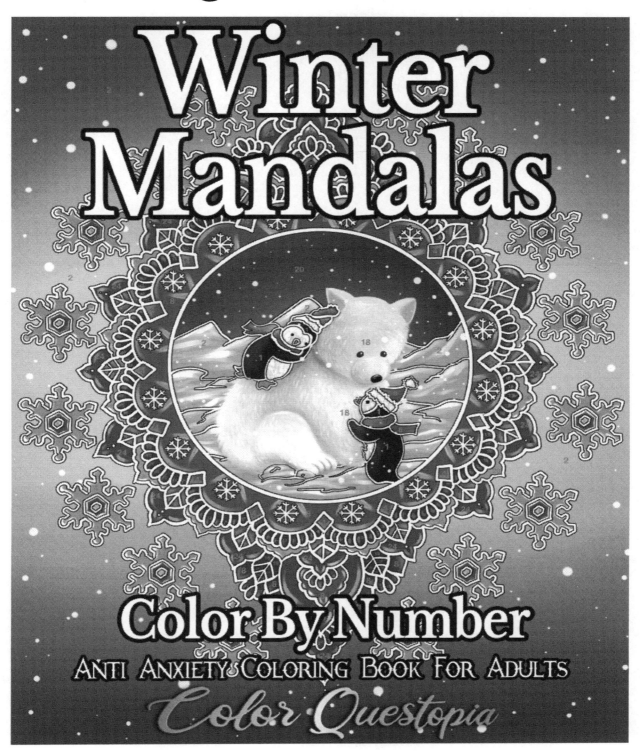

1. Black

2. Gray

4. Brown

5. Dark Brown

6. Tan

8. Red

10. Orange

12. Yellow

14. Light Green

15. Green

17. Aqua Green

18. Light Blue

20. Dark Blue

National Parks
Volume 2
Color By Number
Coloring Book for Adults

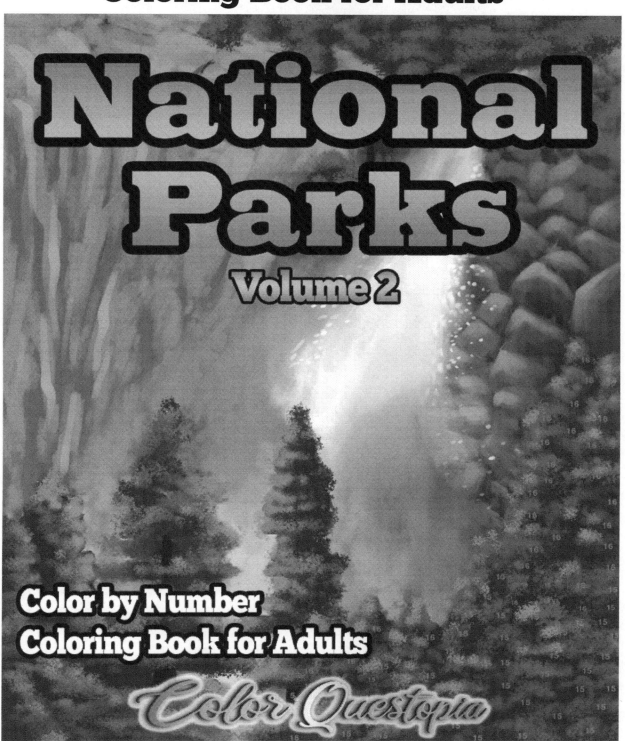

2. Gray

3. Dark Gray

5. Dark Brown

15. Green

16. Dark Green

18. Light Blue

19. Blue

Cuhayoga Valley National Park - Ohio

Interior Design
Color By Number
Adult Coloring Book

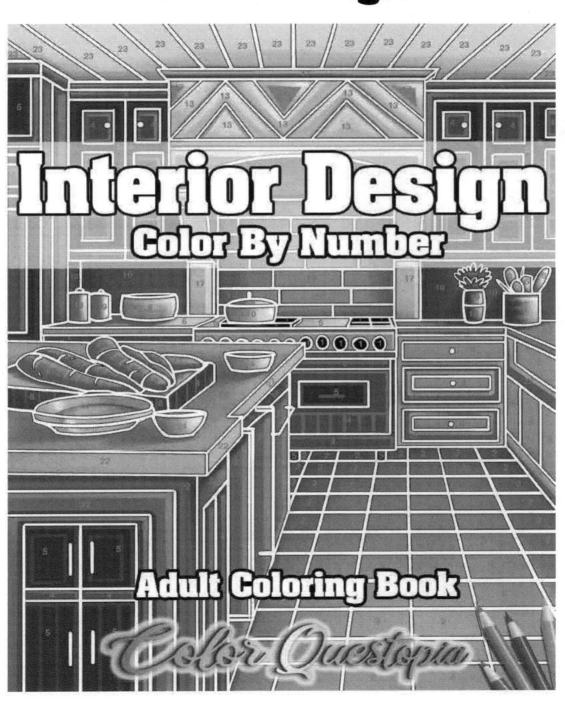

1. Black
2. Gray
3. Dark Gray
4. Brown
5. Dark Brown
6. Tan
7. Peach
8. Red
9. Orange Red
10. Orange
12. Yellow
13. Golden Yellow
15. Green
17. Aqua Green
18. Light Blue

19. Blue
21. Lilac
22. Violet
23. Pink

Custom Color Chart

Medium: _ _ _ _ _ _ _ _   Brand: _ _ _ _ _ _ _ _

1. Black _____
2. Gray _____
3. Dark Gray _____
4. Brown _____

5. Dark Brown _____
6. Tan _____
7. Peach _____
8. Red _____

9. Orange Red _____
10. Orange _____
11. Light Yellow _____
12. Yellow _____

13. Golden Yellow _____
14. Light Green _____
15. Green _____
16. Dark Green _____

17. Aqua Green _____
18. Light Blue _____
19. Blue _____
20. Dark Blue _____

21. Lilac _____
22. Violet _____
23. Pink _____
24. Vivid Pink _____

* Flesh Tone _____

Custom Color Chart

Medium: _____   Brand: _____

1. _____   2. _____   3. _____   4. _____

5. _____   6. _____   7. _____   8. _____

9. _____   10. _____   11. _____   *12. _____

13. _____   14. _____   15. _____   16. _____

17. _____   18. _____   19. _____   20. _____

21. _____   22. _____   23. _____   24. _____

* _____

Color Testing Sheet

Made in the USA
Middletown, DE
24 March 2023

27528277R00051